Dan Burt was born in South Philadelphia in 1942. He attended state schools and a local catholic college before reading English at Cambridge. He graduated from Yale Law School and practiced law in the United States, Saudi Arabia and United Kingdom until moving to London in 1994 and becoming a British citizen. He is an honorary Fellow of St. John's College Cambridge and lives and writes in London. This is his first collection of poems.

To L.B.D., for enduring faith

Dan Burt

Searched for Text

LINTOTT PRESS
Manchester and Glasgow

First published in 2008 by
Lintott Press
Manchester and Glasgow

ISBN 978 1 84777 054 7

Printed and bound in England by SRP Ltd, Exeter

Contents

Modern Painters

Oils are carved, smeared, wrenched to shape,
Black ravines for bones rut a skinless face
Of whites and pewters troweled into place
On an ochre field; canvas then is scraped,
Heaped with paint again, again erased
To make a palimpsest of skin and grace
Until the human mask's at last replaced
With slabs of flesh like a filleted fish.

We look like this after things fall apart;
The painting's just an autopsy report
From an inquest where war took the part
Of coroner. The scalpel lifts to start:
Invade, split rib cage, discard thought and art,
Slit pericardium, examine the heart;
Grab forceps, tear the viscera apart,
That heap of faiths and old philosophies

Covering the mean midden of descent,
Exposing in the entrails of events
Demons Bosch painted and Hobbes penned,
Scenes savage beyond both Testaments
Prophecies. And with dismemberment
A curtain falls on the Enlightenment,
Gone like a *Luftmensch* in the denouement
On the Red march west from Stalingrad.

* See page 32, note 1.

Blue Rinse Matron

A blue rinse matron with her blue rinse friend
Waft down a Maine coast village street.
Her cook hoves into view at the far end
On a course that will see these vessels meet.
Crows' nests register the closing ground,
The lesser craft readies a proper greeting,
But the capital ships wear slowly round
And give their sterns to the tender passing.
Their manoeuvre's not extraordinary,
Logs are full of similar altered courses
To avoid a beggar, mumbling loony
Or ruined friend who once shook bourses:
    Recall the *St. Louis* un-disembarked
    Standing east from Havana into the dark.

* See page 32, note 2.

Wine Circle

Black gowns flap from dinner's tart and cream
To port in Senior Common Room upstairs,
Perch round their Master in the coal fire's gleam
And preen the intellects that bore them there.
They wheel aloft for prey on wings of thought
Above superstition and sentiment,
Dive on topics from maths to art and squawk
As they pick off faulty arguments.
But like us all, falcons wear hoods and wait:
One wants his ashes after death to sit
Potted by his Fellows near the fire grate,
Another found God in a Gobi pit.
The tapers gutter, old birds collapse
Smells of stale wine mingle with melting wax.

Slowly Sounds the Bell

Nunc lento sonitu dicunt, morieris.
Now this bell tolling softly for another, says to me,
Thou must die.

Donne, *Meditation XVII*

A midnight ring from half a world away
Tolls my only brother's sudden death.
Line dead, hand set re-cradled, sleep returns;
I wake to find the bedclothes scarcely mussed.

We long were distant islands to each other -
I stood Esau to his Jacob as a boy,
My fields the sea, his tents the libraries -
DNA proved inadhesive, no gene
Sutured the rifts between us and the news
Was less vexing than a tree fall in my garden.

We hope for more: a foetal element
Feeding fondness for our kin, a shared
Enzyme sealing first cousins best of friends,
From propinquity Gileadan balm:

But boyhood hatred, dumb decades apart
Change blood to water, degauss genealogies:
Abel becomes Cain's pathogen. A shrug
In the cell metastasizes through
Isolate null points of the tribe into
Skull paddies and black snow in June.

Religious tapestries stitched from old deities
Cannot conceal trenches dug between us:
Ancestral chemistry stands hooded on
The scaffold, testing trap and rope for all.

It is the face on the school run who mouths
"Hello", a torso hunched on the next bar stool
Twice a week, a high school sweetheart back,
A man selling ceramics I collect
Dying of AIDS whose curfews heave the clapper
Summoning tears, the shiver in the neck.

Adam's curse is not to scrabble for our bread
But toiling to love others, not wish them dead.

The Lesson

there is not a man in the earth to come in unto us after the
manner of all the earth

Genesis 19:31.

A brimstone stench rises from rotting dead,
Shrouding the salted mother where she stands
On high ground, facing homeward till she melts,
While in a cave her virgin girls assay
The moral smouldering at their backs, and scheme:
"Come, let us make our father drink and we
Will lie with him that we may preserve his seed."

Raw eyed, noses stuffed with sodomites'
And blasphemers' ash, they honor a power
Greater than all there are, and ever were.
Each daughter rapes, each one conceives a child:
The Jordan does not run red, no locusts come,
Their incestuous bellies swell un-condemned.

When seedling cypress crack the lava lid
Tamping bones from Sodom and Gomorrah's dead
Lot's daughters squat on birthing pans
And expel brothers into their father's hands.

Compounds

I

Gone the asphalt soldier
From sand, steppe and polder,
The camps razed or left
Consecrated to death,
The culture shattered
Its thinkers scattered
And flags changed to smoke
From stoves warming the Volk.

II

The feral enterprise put down
What remains of it are nouns
Flung across the fields of thought
Like salt over a barren plot;
Vanilla words for gruesome aims
Like Endlosung and Judenrein –
"Final Solution", "cleansed of Jews" –
"Special detail" for killing crews.

III

The sovereignty of words declines
Through ignorance, distortion, time
Or when the misery they describe
Befalls some other distant tribe:
A pot scorching an infant's hand
Teaches a lesson to the man

His son in turn will have to learn
At a like age, with a like burn.

IV

Tunis rises where Rome sowed
Al Aqsa rests on Temple bones
At Passchendaele the cattle low
In Nagasaki gardens grow:
Ash blackens, rain clears the sky,
Pain ends when the creature dies.

Circumcision

During the Second World War the Nazis often forced men to drop their pants, to check if they were circumcised.

Telushkin, *Jewish Literacy*

Father, grandfathers, great grandfather stand
Round their issue soon to suffer rescission
In an ancient blood rite that leaves a band
Of scar, and him theirs by diminution.
By the door the women of the families
Stand, chattering until their cue to leave
When the knife appears, sugared brandy's
Poured, and talliths cover heads and sleeves.
To dull the pain from the approaching snip
The mohel soaks his finger in the brandy pap
Then gives it as a teat to the initiate
Lying turtled on great-grandpa's lap.
    A wrist flicks, a forebear leans to say
    "For him our suffering began today."

Ishmael

And he will be a wild ass among men, his hand will be
against every man and every man's hand against him.

Genesis 16:12

I

My father fished three days a week,
My mother had a maid to clean and mend,
My brother's hands stayed soft and weak
And I was sent into the cold with men.

Swaddled in a white coat chin to uppers
I trained from twelve to butcher meat
And dress it on enamelled platters
For shoppers shuffling by on sneakered feet;
Played Philoctetes to chicken bones,
Watched a blue line crawl the ulnar vein
And hied septic blood to a ward alone
For antibiotic to remove the stain;
Made green scraps red with nitrate and grinding,
Watched cutting room break men by fifty,
And stood behind a dumpster pissing
To save five minutes when we were busy.

There were no angels in that wilderness
Or wells, no weeping Hagar, no augur
Sifting offal who foretold success
Beyond band saw and block; no wonder
Drug for cleaver blisters or mind gone tough,
No antihistamines to crimp the blush
Raised when the parent of some puppy love
Complained about the sawdust in my cuff.

Memory blackened past reincarnation
I turned my back on home and nation,
Alien now, with alien vision,
Cancers not gone, just in remission.

II

A rusted ring bolt and long length of chain
Lie on the asphalt where a black dog prowls;
The hairless weal around its neck makes plain,
As well as spade ears, fangs, gun barrel snout
That this mailed compound has long been home.
Gates bear no warnings; it has no need to snarl;
Scarred skin, the rasp while gnawing at a bone
Guarantee junked cars in adjacent piles
Rest always undisturbed and rot alone.

Inquisition

I

Sundays they trudged to the Russian baths
(An old trade rite) to steam the stink of fat
From greasy pores, and the chill from bones
Of ice-boxes and concrete floors. Platzas
Done, and mummy-wrapped in cheap thin sheets
Flung over deck chairs from headrests to feet,
They lie in rows like corpses gathered
After a Cossack raid on the Dnieper.

It could have been Odessa, before the war.

Gossip flickers from sweating ghost to ghost -
Futures and unions, money made and lost
How the chains will force them all to the ditch
Whose mother-in-law is the bigger bitch -
But just as grain grinds down a millstone's grooves
The talk comes round to what were Europe's Jews,
English turns to Yiddish, newspapers fall,
Badinage ends, a defendant's called.

It could have been Toledo, without the Cross.

II

Trial begins in time-honoured fashion,
A bencher poses Arendt's question:
"How could you go like cattle to slaughter?"
"Can't you understand" the grey shape mutters,
"We thought we were going to labor camps.

Cheerful cards had come with Polish stamps.
From the platform some went to the 'showers'
After selections, clutching soap and towels."

It could have been Lodz ghetto, without dogs.

He crooks an arm above his head as though
The years have fled before a capo's blow
And unveils a token as sheets fall loose,
Blue faded numbers from a crude tattoo
Done on arrival, each jab in the arm
Tearing the garment that kept the tribe warm
For ages, cut from study, ancient texts,
Faithful heads bowed on stiffened necks.

Der malechamoves oyf a shvartze ferd.

III

Some turn away to rekindle a smoke,
Re-crossing a leg, or slurping a coke
From a dingy half-full cup; no one looks
At the small marks proffered as they mull
The quiet registers of fear, until
Smell of groin and armpit disappeared,
The process continues of finding fault,
Saying these should have run, those should have fought.

It could have been Gehenna, babes and all.

* See page 32, note 3.

Dodge Ball

I

Standing behind a lectern on a milk box
To see above microphones cocked
To catch my words, cornered in a pen
Made from clicking shutters and shouting men,
I lost my way dreaming of Cortez and the sea.
No guide or slave whispered "memento mori",
I never saw the jackals in the shadows
Holding their pens like Herculean arrows
In wait for cripples from that dodge-ball game,
Until a colleague did me like Jesse James.

II

In the Empty Quarter no phones ring
Lunch goes undone, the caravan dwindles.
You sit alone sorting hate mail and bills
For futures bought on notoriety,
Fingering mistakes and credulities
Like a mumbling Bedouin's palsied hand
Telling prayer beads in a dry land.

III

When the dogs and kites rose from their mess
I put down Ecclesiastes, stiffed the press
Stuck poultices to flesh where skin had been
Traded leathers for suits, tucked a foulard in
And walked once more over London Bridge

Into the City.
                    Defeat is a scourge
That changes men: I'm always wary now,
Flinch from compliments, pat each smile down
For the powdered purpose that harbours grief
And welcome old age as a blessed thief
Who will steal me to the dark beyond the need
Of light to read and this damned rage to speak.

Poetry Reading

You turn and face me now
All Bala-Cynwood in your Peter Pan
Collar, and single strand of pearls…
L.E.Sissman, *On The Island*

You turn and face me now
Five feet ten in running
Shoes on the balcony
Of my London hotel
Room, model's form unsexed
By baggy running dress,
Looking incongruous
Dear ageing Irish miss
Reading poems from my
Book open at your waist.

Who would think it's what it
Is, sadly has ever
Been, equilibristic,
Not preface to darting
Tongues and coital bliss,
Merely our mutual
Excuse to lift the scrims
On other poetry
Readings at other trysts?

Facsimile Folio

A blank flyleaf portends pristine leaves
In the Folio you gave me years ago
Exhumed today where it lay un-sleeved
Amongst my present lady's books and clothes.
My fingers trek from first page through to last
(Although I know nothing awaits me there)
Searching for a message that slipped past
Earlier explorations down the years
The way a Qumran scholar's finger scrapes
Encrusted Aramaic scripts for clues
The saviour Jesus Christ, to whom he prays
Was foretold by a splinter sect of Jews.
    That searched for text I shall not find;
    The lines are writ only in my mind.

Winter Mornings

Through frost I navigate Hyde Park
As shapes loom from ebbing dark
When one, red hair drawn back and tied
Above high cheek bones piques my eyes
Which slit to focus. I crane, slack
Way, as last resort change tack
To scout the prize I seem to see.

The western sea splits you from me,
As do your children, husband, faith,
You lie past reach of sail, a wraith.
I know the odds. But still I stare
At a thin stranger walking there,
Like a dawn watch too long at sea
Hailing landfalls that cannot be.

Revenant

For her I did what I had done with others,
Unpicked the cloth woven over years
From wealth and art and anger into armour
Become integument after long wear and tears,
To show her what grief and scorn had fashioned
For armatures to build my masks upon.
What if this autopsy for an old passion
Were to disturb a ghost or raise a storm?
But shaken by her penguin doddle in the snow
And child's smile when she woke to see the dawn
I stammered into silence as she rose,
An iconoclast receding down the lawn,
And toeing fictions shattered at my feet
Watched dust trail her departure through the trees.

Sie Kommt

(...*Es ist die Konigen der Nacht...*)
Tamino, *The Magic Flute* Act 1, sc. 2

She comes with a train of shadows never cast
By any earthly forms whose charge and mass
Thwart light; they flutter just beyond my grasp
Like cherry blossoms a puff of wind unclasps.

She comes around the corner of the years
Streaming faux memories from foreign piers
That never were, dreams I would clear
Of unshared passages, landfalls and tears.

She comes and, for a breath, regret recalls
An unmade voyage: our first-born's squall,
Trimming the sheets while teaching her to sail,
Her hand on mine before my father's pall.

Phantoms swimming in my deeps of night,
No magic flute can pipe you to the light.

End of the Affair

It ends soundlessly: my hand slips yours
To adjust demeanour for a neighbour,
No bang, bombed body sprawled, no prayer,
Just a gentle unlacing of fingers
Tears the tapestry to smithereens we
Fashioned from Fragonards and poetry
To decorate our idyll. We stand
Naked by the roadside, not touching hands,
Sunlit in senescent imperfection -
My stoop and vanished waist, little canyons
Time and disappointment carved from your face -
In silence that surrounds a fall from grace
And separate soon after, sans goodbye,
Relieved that what never lived had died.

Decorating the Nursery

Was I surprised after a year's dispatches
About uxorial combat and its consequences,
Court convoyed visits to your daughter,
Old friendships sunk, financial slaughter
The different mayhem each day brings
When suddenly unbowed, gamboling
You came a-maying with a new consort
Half Venus half Penelope by your report
Who is already "decorating the nursery"
Though no end's in sight to the hostilities?
Not really: consider Chinook perhaps
Leaping water ladders with a tail slap
Scales shimmering rainbow in anticipation
Rushing to their deadly assignation.

Tart

As you descend upon a lady,
The proper sort, not someone shady,
Do you expect a hint of nectar
Or labia a trifle bitter?

I've sampled many I confess
From greedy scrubber to princess,
And must regrettably affirm
Each tasted bitter in her turn.

This evidence compels conviction
That neither birth, nor education,
Nor earthly thing can make one lover
A better dinner than another.

Little Black Dress

My carriage straight, your bosom taut,
I courted you smartly as young men ought,
Applauded your shape in a little black dress,
Followed your arms as they rose to undress.

Now frames are bent, our breastwork sags,
The little black dress is gone for rags
And I court you gently, as old men must,
With a shade less ardour, a bit less fuss.

Un Coup de Des

Chance authors all we do,
The plot's contrived in retrospect.
Spied once I still look out for you;
Chance authors all we do.
A sea bird shot, a woman met
Ungloving who then strolls from view
Alters to fate as we reflect.
Chance authors all we do,
The plot's contrived in retrospect.

Beside a Cove

Beside a cove on the Gulf of Maine
Below a sheer pink granite mountain
Tourists stop where the road flattens
And gaze with natural piety,
No sighs, no trembling
For nature as a darkening thing.

And though not reverent I too
Sometimes halt and stare at that view,
Until mountain seems air not rock
And sea time, setting all to be
With all I see toward nullity,
No light, no land, oceans become
Stray particles near a dead sun,
Then with a nod walk on.

Notes

1   p. 7, "Modern Painters": Death camp inmates made ironic and literal use of the Yiddish word "Luftmensch", meaning an unworldly, contemplative and impractical man, to refer to the ashes of cremated victims exiting the crematoria smoke stacks.

2   p. 8, "Blue Rinse Matron": The SS *St. Louis* left Hamburg on May 13, 1939 carrying 1000 Jews fleeing Germany. Cuba and the US refused to permit the *St. Louis*'s passengers to disembark, and on June 7th the ship turned back to Europe where many of its passengers eventually were murdered.

3   p. 18, "Inquisition": A "platza" is a massage and cleansing administered with a soapy oak brush in a dry steam room. The practice originated in Russia and was brought to the West by Jewish working class immigrants who visited "the schvitz" weekly when they lived in the Pale of Settlement.

The platza-man stands on a bench above the client, who lies face down on a bench higher than and stepped back from the bench on which the platza-man is standing. He wears a cloth cap under which he stuffs a hose running cold water as he massages and scrubs the client, gradually increasing the heat in the platza room till the client can bear no more.

The client then is helped out of the platza room to an adjacent shower stall where he takes an ice cold shower and then immediately reclines on a deck chair while he is wrapped head to toe in towels and cotton sheets to continue sweating. Men may lie for several hours sweating and talking to other men "having a sheet wrap" after "taking a platza."

The Inquisition Tribunal was established in Toledo in 1485. Twenty-five *auto de fes* were held in Toledo between 1485 and 1492, and 467 *conversos* were burned at the stake, alive. (Jewish Virtual Library, *The Inquisition*)

The Lodz ghetto was one of the largest in the *Generale Gouvernement*, producing manufactures for the German war effort. All of its inhabitants were transported over two years to the death camp at Chelmno and gassed, the last of them in June, 1944. The transportees were told they were being sent to munitions factories in Germany.

Day to day affairs in the Lodz ghetto were run by a *Judenrat*, or Jewish Council, whose president was the notorious Chaim Rumkowski, "King of the Jews" who went to his death still protesting that by cooperating with the Germans at least some would be saved. His Jewish police were known for their ferocity in forcing Jews to obey their captors.

Der malechamoves oyf a schvartze ferd was a common term for a terrible person or thing among Yiddish speaking peasants in the Pale. It means "the angel of death on a black horse" and suggests the idol Moloch, to whom babies were sacrificed at Gehenna by the Canaanites and, some scholars believe, the early Hebrews.